the catalog of daily fears
© Beth Dufford / Cathexis Northwest Press

No part of this book may be reproduced without written permission of the
publisher or author, except in reviews and articles.

First Printing: 2022

Paperback ISBN: 978-1-952869-62-4

Cover art by C. M. Tollefson
Designed and edited by C. M. Tollefson

Cathexis Northwest Press
cathexisnorthwestpress.com

the catalog of daily fears

poetry by Beth Dufford

Beth Dufford's poems frame our fears as well as the terror *we are still collectively ok with*. With stark humor and steep enjambments, the poems' titles, tonal shifts, size and shape make news of spells, missing women, domestic violence, war, religion, surveillance, protests and political financiers all feel like a scroll through your favorite media feed. "Because So Much Has Been Sold in the Name of Convenience" *if you zoom out far enough* [our fear] *seems really small.*

Valyntina Grenier, author of *In Our Now* and *Fever Dream/Take Heart*

The Faults Are Being Manufactured Using Our Own Co-opted Factories

since we tell ourselves
    we knew this is how it would be

since we carry cardboard and
    nod when someone points out her warnings

since we stopped
    paying close-close attention

and since then, the bombs got quieter, too

and because crows can recognize human faces as
    well as any modern city lamppost can

because we're entirely
    convinced we're good

because if we're not
    than who?

because all this shame is ours

It Only Takes Two Decades
to Accept Constant Conflict

after the last patient, rocking,
    smokes his last

after he reaches across time
    and lights one for the infantryman

after the call to prayer
    no longer echoes

after the phone is hung up

and because our calves ache
    from a desert hike

because you never think you're
    ever enough

because you are soft and grasp fistfuls
    of oatmeal and shame

because even the sun is complicit in setting

And What We Learned Overnight
Will Be Eclipsed by Noon

when it comes to fall, with its withering and
    dying biomass, falling

when piles of the formerly green and
    chlorophyll-infused amass

when notebooks are new and
    pages unfilled

when all this is happening, how can we keep track?

if notes are taken
    and burned

if notes exist
    in secret, invisible notebooks

if notes aren't taken
    if notes aren't notes

if leaves are further entombed in the first of months of snow

Because He Will Fill a Moot with Alligators and Misunderstood Precedents

because you remained at your post
despite your *compadres* being ordered to stand down

because their commander is a whirligig with
arms a-spin, mouth agape

because their commander's constituency
would sooner die than admit to pissing with fear

because these are other people; dirty, they

and because sausages are tasty
and the meat smells good grilled

if there's time and space enough to
enjoy it all, consume it

if we continue to create memorials
only to the richest of our rapists

because to measure return, you have to count the bullets

We Will Drown Ourselves in the Relative Comfort of Our Own Homes

because this pig only stands for snacks
and feasts on loose-knit fears

because this pig snuggles the old and
sprinkles yesterdays on their coffeecake

since I can't tell you not to chant your spells and
because I won't trample your rights

because this pig farts and says it's snorting

because I'm only brave every other Tuesday and
even when the brackish murk recedes   still

if I could hold your hoof and
you could hold my paw, still

if we whisper *non plus*
but wait too long

although we whisper *no mas*

Which We Will Lose

because there are so many conflicting opinions about
    the apocalypse

because we're still individually shocked by what
    people are collectively okay with

because coconut sunscreen wafts and
    cigarette butts soak up the soda in the bottom of the can

if the erasures hasten

and if anticipating this dog's demise
    continues to elicit a yawn

if we all can't spit out
    our most corrosive thoughts

if the sight of something crawling yellow-spotted and naked on
    this forest floor ceases to cause momentary wonder

and if the erasures leave no shadows

Because Someone Applauded the News Cycle About a Girl Whose Parents Were Disappeared

because it's October
       we've forgotten

because everyone is tired
       and everyone _____

because how can anyone
       keep up; can anyone keep up?

if we are like water will we succeed?

if someone got the glees from
       a girl coming home to an empty house

if someone got high off her realization
       they had disappeared

because it was the first day of school
       and her mom kissed her and wished her luck and

if you zoom out far enough, it seems really small

Truth is Measured Using a Yardstick Made of Frankfurters

when we start to measure
        truth with elaborate pulley systems

when we use a yardstick
        made of link sausages

and when a cartoon dog
        runs behind the truth apparatus

and if he scarfs each link as soon as it hits the ground

when we continue
        to laugh until we don't

when we laugh and laugh and
        dress up for TV dance time

when we draw a cartoon dog and
        it comes to life wearing a cartoon bowler

and when he sends a horseshoe wreath of roses to our funeral

And This Is Us

if we let it
   just end

if we do not reflect
   on big numbers

if we serve only the wiltiest
   of the red cabbage slivers

and if we ignore the bright pink streaky sunsets

because the flood waters of
   San Marco deter the pigeons

because we love our
   avocado with a wedge of lemon

and if bright pink
   streaky sunsets make us sigh

because we'd rather kill it than share it

He'll Say He's Sorry; We'll Believe Him

though we saw
what we saw

because mocha
latte wool

though we know
what we know

because jam toast butter

because his friends and family
are both dumb

though we learn about
new facts, new history

though we watched her
recount humiliation on TV

because we will absolve them so that we may absolve us

We Will Cling to Plausible Deniability for Another Four Hundred Years

because what if
  it's not his fault?

because a collection of
  sippy cups is called a "chaos"

because shouting over a chopper
  happens in war movies

because not all _____ people are bad

and if small bits of orange
  pulp cling to the sides of a cup

and if they wave Photoshopped pictures
  of fictitious muscle men

and if we decide
  to forgive ourselves without trial

because it was the 1600s and I wasn't even born

And She'll Spend Her Advance on a Fence Around Her House

because they weren't burned,
    they were hung

because their torture
    is our shorthand—wtchnt

because also:
    they were pressed to death

because sink/float is still a test

and if
she floats

if she floats
she loses

if stakes are high,
we make them higher

and when they sing, we jail them

A Large Percentage of Missing Women
Fit through Missing Women-shaped Cracks

even though, low carb or no,
  it may not fit your lifestyle

because no matter how little,
  no one wants to see them

because if you can't take a joke,
  I was only kidding

if the crack fits

because fat
  is fat free

if fat is free, why
  am I not?

if all women are
  good women

if a large percentage of missing women are missing

And We Wonder How
Any of This Will Ever Be Funny?

although: funny
  is subjective

although some of us
  can breathe enough to laugh

when we measure
  strength over time

if we squint, it's not so bad

if we spare ourselves
  looking at ourselves

when you say
  oh, spare me and roll your eyes

if so much
  depends upon a chicken sandwich

if I comply, I comply

We've Been Pretending
Such a Long While Now

if we glom onto the saying
   left a lot of egg in the pan

when we accept the blame
   for our welts

if a man is strong
   he is a strong man

if a woman is strong, she she she she she

when dismissing
   exquisite intelligence

when accepting
   imminent threats

if unfit, they remain
   bathed in light and untethered

if fit, sh sh sh sh sh

"The Panic Going on in Some Circles is Really Something to See"

if only in reaction
    to some other, stale panic

if in the parlance
    of food snobs in the know

if blind to the
    gift of clean water

and if the search knows all of this

even though
    the low hum panic

(because the panic
    is only present in some circles)

even though everyone knows
    a handful of chia seeds is called a "remark"

and even though the panic seeps out everywhere in shrieks and squeaks

Please Indicate You've Read Our Terms and Conditions

even if you
    love cats

even if you
    loved *Cats*

even though
    you don a leopard print

and if you believe all squirrels are not equal

if her
    DNA is called "exotic"

if you know that
    a jeans pocket full of tahini is called a "trimester"

if the monotony fits,
    swear it

if your toaster
    has a privacy waiver

and if you read it and wondered: are my sobs electric?

Because So Much Has Been Sold
in the Name of Convenience

if you are
    in the shade of a granite skyscraper

when you are
    nursing a dread of cilantro

if all the terms
    are conditional

and if you know what a good bake looks like

and if your warm
    wishes are, in truth, lukewarm

and if the art of the hissy fit
    is tiresome

and if you cradle
    your caring deeply

when only 3.5% on our feet is rumored to be effective

We'll Wake Up and
Most of It Will Have Vanished

although we whisper *no mas;*
because even the sun is complicit in setting

if leaves are further entombed in the first of months of snow
because you are awake and you think you are alive

because to measure return, you have to count the bullets
because all this shame is ours, shared

and if the erasures leave no shadows

and if you zoom out far enough, it seems really small

Addendum

the faults are being manufactured with our own co-opted factories
it only takes twenty years to accept constant conflict
and what we learned overnight will be eclipsed by noon
because he will fill a moot with alligators and misunderstood precedents
we will drown ourselves in the relative comfort of our own homes
which we will lose
because someone applauded a news cycle about a girl whose parents were disappeared
truth is measured using a yardstick made of frankfurters
and this is us
he'll say he's sorry; we'll believe him
we will cling to plausible deniability for another four hundred years
and she'll spend her advance on a fence around her house
a large percentage of missing women fit through missing women-shaped cracks
and we wonder how any of this will ever be funny
we've been pretending such a long time now
the panic going on in some circles is really something to see
please indicate you've read our terms and conditions
because so much has been sold in the name of convenience
we'll wake up and most of it will have vanished

Also Available
from
Cathexis Northwest Press:

Cathexis Northwest Press

CPSIA information can be obtained
at www.ICGtesting.com
Printed in the USA
BVHW011643270622
640731BV00009B/121

9 781952 869624